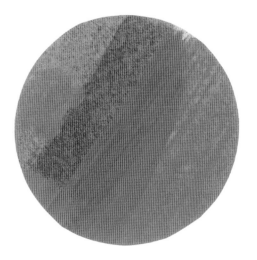

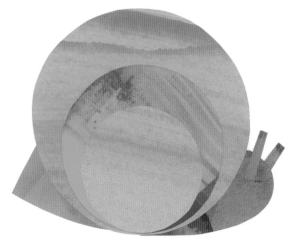

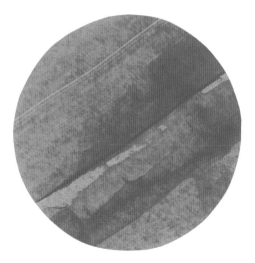

For Dad

Library of Congress Cataloging-in-Publication Data available.

ISBN 978-1-7972-2018-5

Manufactured in China.

Design by Jay Marvel.
Typeset in Brown.
The illustrations in this book were cut and collaged
from hand-painted paper and then assembled digitally.

10 9 8 7 6 5 4 3 2 1

Chronicle Books LLC
680 Second Street
San Francisco, California 94107

Chronicle Books—we see things differently.
Become part of our community at www.chroniclekids.com.

some of these are snails

carter higgins

chronicle books · san francisco

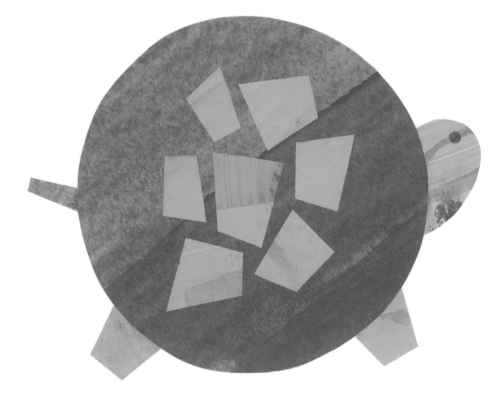

turtle is a circle

circle is a snail

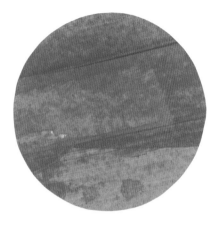

green circles

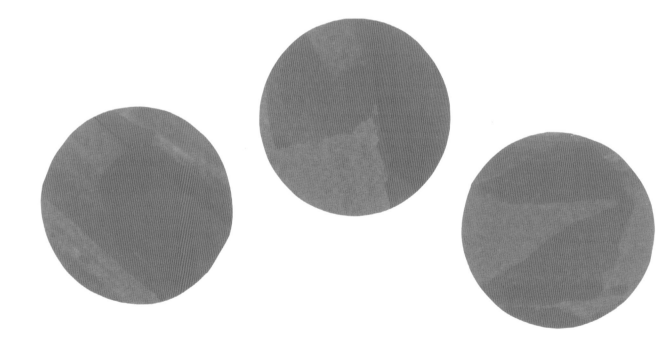

orange circles

circle circle square

yellow is an elephant

owl is a square

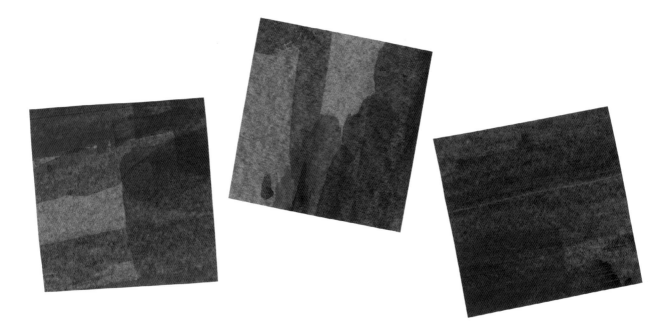

yellow squares

blue squares

owl yellow snail

purple circles

small circles

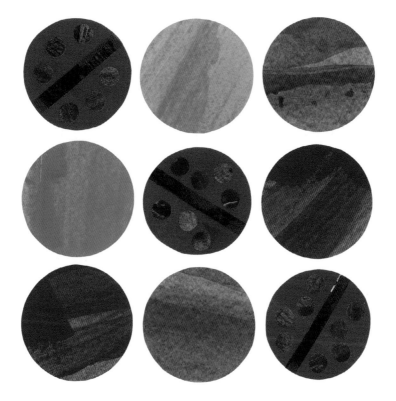

circles in a square

big squares

red squares

square is a whale

can you sort by color?

can you sort by size?

can you sort by shape or find the animals with eyes?

all of these are triangles
all of these are pink
some of them go
tweet-tweet-tweet
some of them go squeak

**all of these are ovals
three of them are bees**

some of these are octagons
two of those are green

all the ladybugs have spots

each butterfly has none

this tiger has a lot of stripes

this tiger has just one

what is one?
what is some?
where is all and
where is none?

who's stripiest?
who's spottiest?

who's wiggly wigglier wiggliest?

one of these is purple

some of these are snails

all of these are circles

none of these are squares

big bigger biggest
owl square purple

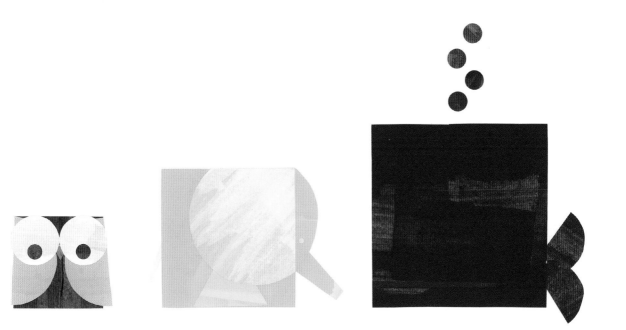

small smaller smallest
orange turtle circle

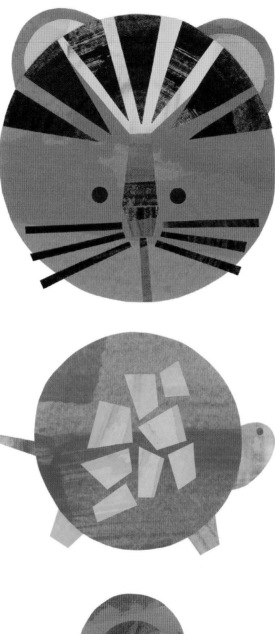

little bitty ladybugs

huge enormous snails

teeny tiny elephants

giant mighty whales

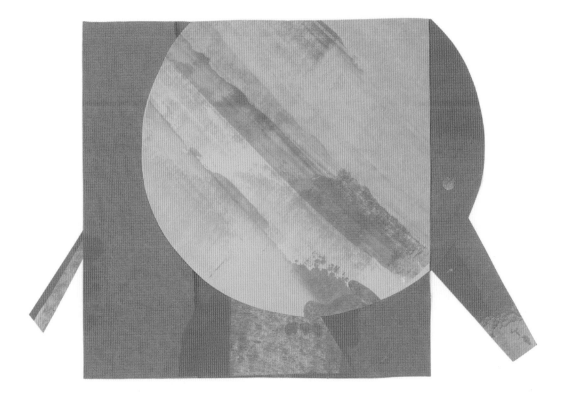

orange is an elephant

owl is a square

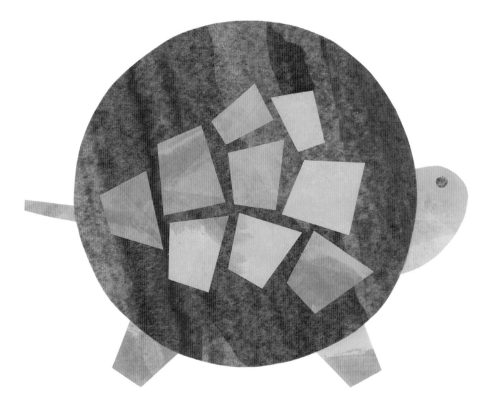

turtle is a circle

circle is a snail

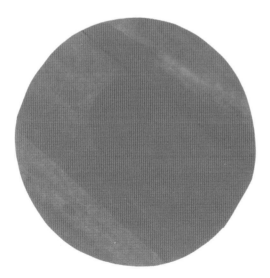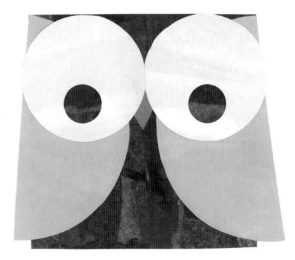